DOLCE ITALIA

Authentic Italian Baking

By Damiano and Massimiliano Carrara

ISBN: 978-1-4834-4326-3 (sc)
ISBN: 978-1-4834-4325-6 (e)

Library of Congress Control Number: 2015920545

Lulu Publishing Services rev. date: 1/26/2016

INTRODUCTION

Let me start by thanking everyone who made this book a reality--all the people that support us, as well as all the family members that encourage us. I feel very proud and blessed for all the accomplishments I have made during my life. My journey started back in Italy in a small village called Sant'Angelo in Campo, located in the city of Lucca, Italy.

Growing up in the countryside of Tuscany, I was surrounded by fresh ingredients from nature. Across the street from my house, we had a beautiful garden filled with fresh strawberries, plums, peaches, pears, along with several other fruits, and vegetables. On the side of the house, we had pigs, cows, all the fresh milk that you could think of, and a small henhouse with chickens and fresh farm eggs. My family never really baked except for special occasions, but I remember two things: my mom picking up fresh eggs from the farm and us eating those eggs, beaten with sugar or fresh vanilla custard, after school. The entire house always smelled like fresh vanilla, and those memories will never be forgotten. My mom, Laura, works at the post office, and my dad was a contractor and built houses. Several days a week, my dad, Ivano, and my grandpa left town and went to work in a small village called Pianaccio in the mountain near Bologna, where we still have a beautiful house.

In Pianaccio, I met Gianni, the owner of a small restaurant, who taught me how to make our delicious Gelato alla Crema (vanilla custard gelato).

Growing up in Italy, I remember my brother Massimiliano skipping school to go fulfill his passion. My family thought he was in school. Instead, he was learning how to create delicious pastries and gelato at Le Bonta', the pastry shop where he was working. He was our little genius, learning how to bake and coming back home to try the recipes for all the goodies he had learned to make. I remember him at a very young age attempting to mix eggs with flour and his baking all sorts of things which were a little bit messy. I will say, my Grandma Rosita was always there next to him. My grandma makes one of my favorite desserts of all time: a cake soaked with Alkermes liqueur filled with cream and chocolate. Every holiday and family reunion, she prepared it, and we all enjoyed it. Grazie, Nonna, for all the sweet memories I have of you!

Eventually, Massimiliano's passion, with the help of the pastry chefs working next to him, enabled him to learn the recipes and the techniques that brought us here. On the other side, I was working as a metal mechanic in a big factory in Lucca. My passion for cooking then forced me to quit my job, and I decided to leave my sweet home of Italy and go to Dublin, Ireland.

Life in Dublin was really hard, especially because my English was not even close to understandable. Slowly, I managed to start understanding people and to have little conversations. Thanks to that, I found a job in the middle of the city in a prestigious Italian restaurant called Town Bar & Grill where I worked as a bartender. With a job in the restaurant business, I learned how to handle customers, bring glasses to the tables, clean tables, and manage all the duties of working the front of the house. Home was far away, as well as all my family, and the different culture did not make it easy for me to stay. After a year of hard work, I decided to return home. Immediately after getting home, I met my mentor, Mauro Picchi, also known as the prince of the bar. He taught me everything I know about bartending and serving. Grazie, Mille Mauro sei il Migliore!!!!

Anyway, after my experience abroad, life in Italy was pretty boring. My brother was still working at Le Bonta' di Lucca, the same pastry shop where he was hired at the age of 14, and I was working as a bartender with Mauro in a beautiful place in the middle of Lucca. Things were good back home, but for me that wasn't enough. I then decided to leave again and go to America, which at the time, was like a faraway place, impossible to reach.

Getting to America: the culture, as well as the good in the people, impressed me, and right away, I loved the beauty of this place. Thanks to Mauro, I once again found a place to work. I took a job with Jacopo Falleni, a graduate from the same bartending school I had attended. Jacopo owned Cafe Firenze across the street from where my pastry shop eventually opened in December 2011. Working in America, my brother's and my dream was to finally bring our passions together. I was an expert in the front of the house, and he was the expert in the kitchen. We decided to save our money and open our little store, called Carrara Pastries.

Running a pastry business is different from working in a restaurant, so my brother started training me as a pastry chef, too. I've learned so much, and everything I know I give credit to my brother. We then opened a second store in Agoura Hills, California, and right after that, we expanded our first location. Our Moorpark store now serves fresh gelato, panino, salad, pasta, as well as our handmade, one-of-a-kind pastries and cakes. My brother and I spend every day at our stores; this industry is our passion, and we will continue working hard in order to share good, authentic Italian food with as many people as possible.

We have now been in business for four years, and we decided to share some of our best family recipes with you. We hope you will enjoy this book the same way we enjoy baking these recipes every day. Baking, for us, is a lifestyle, a way of thinking, and a precise art that satisfies all!!! If you follow our recipes, you will be discovering the flavour of our land and will immerse yourself into a journey through Italian culture!!!!

BIOGRAPHY

DAMIANO CARRARA

Damiano Carrara was born in 1985 in Lucca, Tuscany, in a small village called Sant'Angelo in Campo in the Italian countryside.

Growing up, Damiano developed an interest in the restaurant world and, at a young age, began his career in his own town, bartending in a place called Happy Days. From there, he moved to Dublin, Ireland, where he continued working as a bartender and learned new techniques. One year later, he moved back to Italy where he began his professional bartending training with AIBES (Italian Bartender Association) and eventually graduated with a mixology certificate. Shortly after, he started training as a flair bartender, spending half-days training for competition. Flair bartending is the exciting juggling of bartending tools to entertain customers. Soon, Damiano was competing in such cities as Switzerland, Paris, Florence, and Milano. While he was working as a bartender during this time, he also taught flair bartending in Pontedera, Pisa. He then joined the FBA (Flair Bartenders' Association) and decided to move to America.

Damiano's first job in the United States was at an Italian restaurant, Cafe Firenze, working as a bartender, and he competed in flair bartending competitions in Arizona, Las Vegas, and San Diego, winning multiple awards, including World Finalist, Kahunaville Island Restaurant, Treasure Island Hotel and Casino, Las Vegas; third place, Firestarter Competition; first place, Jim Beam competition, Las Vegas; first place, San Diego competition; and World finalist, Paris Flair Open.

Taking the opportunity to grow, Damiano started managing Café Firenze, as well. During this period, he decided to start his own business with his brother, Massimiliano. In 2011, after five years of hard work, he opened Carrara Pastries in Moorpark, California, that specializes in Italian pastries, coffee, gelato, panini, wine, beer and so much more. After positive feedback from press and media, the success of the first store led to the opening of Carrara Pastries in Agoura Hills, California, in 2013. In 2015, after training with his brother as a pastry chef, Damiano participated in the Food Network's Spring Baking Championship television show where he made it to the final round followed by a huge response from the public. Currently, Damiano and his brother Massimiliano are working on expanding production and opening new locations.

MASSIMILIANO CARRARA

Massimiliano Carrara was born in 1987 and is the brother of Damiano. The Carrara Pastries pastry chef, Massimiliano, is a native from the city of Lucca, Tuscany, and is renowned in his country after graduating from the Italian Academy of Master Pastry Chefs in the Italian town of Rimini. He has practiced his passion for cake creations for over 10 years and has perfected the arts of both chocolate sculpting and sugar-pulling techniques.

PHOTOGRAPHER
Tony McNamara

Tony has been a Director/Cinematographer in advertising for over 30 years. His love for still photography, combined with the beauty of the Carrara brothers beautiful creations, resulted in the images for this book.

We would like to thank the following people and family members for the realization of this book. Please, if we forget someone, don't take it personally. Sometimes we make mistakes too! Thank you to mom, Laura; father, Ivan; wife Joanna, Grandma Rosita; Grandpa Romano; Grandma Liliana; Grandpa Osvaldo; Great Aunt Magda; Uncle Vincenzo; Aunt Luana; cousin Chiara; cousin Martina; Uncle Gianfranco; Aunt Marisa; cousin Alessandro; Aunt Lia; cousin Ilaria and her husband, Marco, and all the kids; Uncle Stefano and Aunt Luisa and cousins Samuele and Lorenzo. Thank you, Rebecca at Flower Power Studios for the beautiful flowers in the photographs. Thank you to Apricot Lane Farms in Moorpark, CA for the beautiful backdrop and your fresh farm eggs. Thanks to Tony for his incredible photos. Thank you to Linda Olson for your contributions, time, and editing of this book. And thanks to Jocelyn Peterson for testing the recipes in this book.

A huge thank you to all my employees of the past and present, along with the managers: Daniel Alvarez, Shaylee Olson, Francesco Colistra, and Diego Cruz. Really, without you guys, this would have been impossible. Grazie!!!

Grazie to all our close friends Lo Zio, Il Del Bianco, lo scemo del Cannella, Jonathan (Il miccio), Puffo o l'elfo, il Mobi, Iacopo, Il pazzo dello Stagi, Il Rosa, Tatonno, Bruno Bruni, Il dottor Francesco Colistra, Fabio Vota, Il natucci.

CONTENTS

BASIC RECIPES

CREAMS AND CUSTARDS

COTTI IN FORNO (COOKED IN THE OVEN)

PASTICCERIA MIGNON (BITE-SIZED PASTRIES)

L'ARTE DEL GELATO (ART OF GELATO)

RICETTE DI FAMIGLIA (CARRARA FAMILY RECIPES)

"00" FLOUR

If you want to use a flour that has the silkiness of talcum powder, use "00" flour. This is the highest refined Italian flour, and it yields the best results.

At the far end of the range, Italian grade 2 flour is wholemeal and contains the highest level of germ and bran. Ranging from grade "2," the milling process further refines wheat berries to "1," "0" and "00" grades. As the most refined, "00" flour contains the least amount of germ and bran, but the highest level of protein. Italian baking features "00" flour in pizza dough, pasta, and gnocchi recipes.

While the recipes in this book call for "00" flour, an equal amount of unbleached, all-purpose flour or cake flour can be used as a substitute.

ALKERMES LIQUEUR

The creation of the Alkermes liqueur seems to be the telling of a fairy tale. This sweet, red liqueur was created by monks in Florence, Italy, as early as the 15th century. The monks lived and worked at the Santa Maria Novella basilica in a converted cloister that functioned as an apothecary--what is now considered one of the oldest pharmacies in the world.

The pharmacy, originally a workshop for creating health remedies, eventually became known for its perfumes and liqueurs. The pharmacy's fame was solidified in the 1600s when the monks created a fragrance to celebrate the marriage of fourteen-year-old Catherine de Medici's wedding. The Medici family particularly liked Alkermes liqueur, and the recipe was finally recorded in 1743 by Fra Cosimo Bucelli, then director of the pharmacy.

Alkermes liqueur is made from extracts of herbs and spices such as rose water, orange blossom water, cinnamon, vanilla, nutmeg, and coriander. The ruby color comes from crushed cochineal, or ladybugs. The red color gives the liqueur its name, from the Arabic word "qirmiz," meaning "of scarlet color."

Santa Maria Novella liqueurs and fragrances are still in production today, and the Santa Maria Novella church is currently open as a museum.

HOW TO READ THE RECIPES

Let me start by saying what baking means to us. Baking is a lifestyle of passion, accuracy, technique and precision. Everything we ever learned from the best pastry chefs in the world is that you can't bake without weighing your products. A small mistake in the recipe will result in an unsuitable final product, imbalanced in flavor. All our recipes are measured in grams or liters, which are much easier to scale and to multiply or divide. Baking demands precision, so we MUST scale every little ingredient that goes into making your dessert. We have included conversions into American standard measurements; however, we strongly encourage you to use a scale for each recipe.

TOOLS IN THE KITCHEN

Baking Sheets
Bowl, steel with handle and thick bottom
Convection Oven
Cookie Cutters (In different sizes)
Flame Torch
Immersion Blender
Metal Cylinders
Mixer (with hook and paddle attachment)
Pastry Bag with Metal Tips
Pastry Rings
Saucepan
Scale
Scraper
Spatula
Rolling Pin
Sieve
Thermometer with probe
Whisk
8-inch Cake Pan – Tart Pan
9-inch Cake Pan – Tart Pan

BASIC RECIPES

This chapter will give you the skills and understanding of how to successfully create incredible Italian pastries fit for any occasion. These recipes are the base for count-less possibilities of what you can make. Pies, tarts, cakes, cookies, and cream puffs: these are traditional Italian recipes that any chef, at any skill level, can create.

PAN DI SPAGNA (sponge cake)

Pan di Spagna is a dessert that, from the moment of its creation by a very Italian chef, has entered into everyday baking. Its appearance is as distinctive as its taste: soft, gold-colored, delicately perfumed, gently spongy.

VANILLA BEAN SEEDS, extracted 1 pod
EGGS 5
SALT 1 pinch
SUGAR 150 g (½ cup + 1 tbsp)
"00" FLOUR 75 g (½ cup)
POTATO STARCH 75 g (½ cup + 1 tbsp)
Option: add orange zest to recipe.

To prepare the sponge cake, cut vanilla bean and remove seeds. Combine eggs, pinch of salt, sugar and vanilla bean seeds (option: flavour additionally with orange zest). Whip for at least 10 minutes at medium speed until mixture is puffy, light, and fluffy. Add sifted flour and potato starch. Fold into egg mixture with a spatula very carefully from the bottom to the top, making sure the air in the mixture doesn't disappear.

Grease and flour a 9-inch pan if you want a high sponge cake (otherwise use a 10-inch pan for a larger, slightly lower cake) and pour in the mixture. Flatten the batter with a spatula. Bake at 350°F for 30-35 minutes. Once the sponge cake is cooked, remove from oven and let it cool. Remove from pan and serve it or stuff it!!

PASTA FROLLA (shortbread)

Shortbread is a versatile base for excellent desserts. It is a cornerstone of pastry and very simple to make. Learn to make it, and you will enjoy many delicious desserts!

UNSALTED BUTTER, cubed 150 g (¾ cup)
POWDERED SUGAR 100 g (¾ cup)
EGG YOLKS 2
"00" FLOUR 300 g (2 cups)
LEMON ZEST ½ lemon
VANILLA EXTRACT 1 tsp

In a mixing bowl, use a hook attachment to combine cubed butter and powdered sugar. Mix at lowest speed. Once the butter and sugar are fully combined, add egg yolks.

Incorporate the flour all at once and mix to perfection. Flavour, finally, the pastry with lemon zest and vanilla extract (or vanilla). Turn out the dough onto a work surface and knead quickly. Mash dough into a disc and wrap in waxed paper. Let it cool down in the refrigerator and then use it as you like to make cookies, tarts, and more.

GENOISE

With this recipe you will be able to create a thin layer of sponge cake which will allow you to roll it and build a layered cake.

> **EGGS, ROOM TEMPERATURE 5**
> **SUGAR 175 g (¾ cup)**
> **VANILLA BEAN SEEDS, extracted**
>   **1 pod**
> **SALT 1 pinch**
> **UNSALTED BUTTER, melted 80 g**
>   **(¼ cup)**
> **"00" FLOUR 100 g (½ cup)**

Pour the eggs into a mixing bowl. Add sugar, vanilla bean seeds scraped from the pod, and pinch of salt. Mix at medium-to-high speed for at least 8 minutes while warming the outside of the bowl with a flame torch without burning the batter. This will allow our ingredients to rise and to incorporate air, which is the most important part of our sponge.

Sift flour into the mixture, folding gently. Take out 10 percent of the mixture and combine it with melted butter (butter needs to be liquid but not hot). Once the butter is combined, finish by folding into the rest of the mixture. Pour our genoise onto a sheet pan previously oiled and lined with parchment paper. Using a spatula, spread sponge into a thin layer and cook in the oven at 450°F for 4-5 minutes.

CHOCOLATE SPONGE CAKE

The chocolate sponge cake is one of the variants of the traditional sponge cake: sweet, tasty, and widely used in pastry. It is the ideal base to prepare delicious cakes and can be filled with any type of cream, such as milk or the classic custard, which enhances the flavor nicely.

EGG YOLKS 230 g (12 yolks)
SUGAR 200 g (1 cup)
LEMON ZEST ½ lemon
VANILLA BEAN SEEDS, extracted 1 pod
SALT 1 pinch
SUGAR 50 g (¼ cup)
EGG WHITES 250 g (8 whites)
SIFTED "00" FLOUR 50 g (⅓ cup)
POTATO STARCH 50 g (⅓ cup)
COCOA POWDER 50 g (⅓ cup)
UNSALTED BUTTER, melted 100 g (½ cup)

Beat egg yolks with sugar, aroma (lemon zest and vanilla), and salt. Whip sugar with egg whites until creamy. Delicately combine one part of egg white-and-yolk mixture with a part of the sifted powders (flour, potato starch, cocoa powder). Repeat until done. Take out ¹⁄₁₀ of the mix and incorporate melted butter gently. Then fold back into the rest of the batter. Pour mix into a buttered 9-inch pan and cook right away at 350°F for 25-30 minutes in a convection oven.

PÂTE À CHOUX

This is one of our favourite desserts to make because it is the perfect base of the profitterole and many other desserts. Filling the pâte à choux with cream is what makes this dessert so good. The merit of such goodness goes to the choux pastry, a basic preparation, light and delicate, a neutral mixture to be stuffed with delicious creams or to be made as a savory version for a gourmet buffet! In the oven, choux pastry becomes puffed and dry, taking the classic form of cream puffs, or small "choux," which in French means "cabbage." The pastry puffs are named "choux" because the shape resembles Brussels sprouts. Discover, step-by-step, how to get a perfect choux pastry to create delicious recipes.

WATER 200 ml (1 cup)
UNSALTED BUTTER cubed 100 g (½ cup)
SALT 1 pinch
"00" FLOUR 125 g (¾ cup)
EGGS 4-5

Bring the water, cubed butter, and salt to a boil in a saucepan. Add flour all at once. Cook to dry the mixture, stirring briskly, until a tight dough forms and pulls away from the pan. Pour the mixture in a mixing bowl with a paddle attachment. Incorporate eggs slowly, 1 by 1. Place round half-balls on a greased pan using a pastry bag. Bake for 15 minutes at 350°F or until golden. Now your pâte à choux is ready. You can use it right away to make éclairs, cream puffs, and more delicious desserts!

GLUTEN-FREE CHOCOLATE SPONGE CAKE

This is a very creative and unique recipe. A chocolate sponge cake without any gluten will need something to keep it up. The air created from whipping the eggs is what will make the sponge stay up. In order to successfully execute this, you will need to avoid over-whipping the eggs and to very delicately fold in all the other ingredients.

EGG WHITE 300 g (9 egg whites)
SUGAR 100 g (½ cup)
EGG YOLKS 75 g (2 yolks)
MELTED UNSALTED BUTTER 70 g (⅓ cup)
MELTED DARK CHOCOLATE 350 g (1 ¼ cup)

Whip egg yolks and sugar together until creamy. Melt butter and dark chocolate, once they are melted. After chocolate is slightly cooled, add to egg yolk mixture. Whip egg whites until stiff peaks form. Slowly incorporate egg whites into your mixture. Pour into a greased 8-inch pan (9-inch pan if you want a thinner cake). Bake at 350°F for 20-30 minutes.

BISCOTTI AL CIOCCOLATO

This is one of the most renowned cookies that comes from Italy. Because you can find several different recipes for this cookie, we decided to make a variation and make a very nice chocolate and pistachio biscotti.

PISTACHIO NUTS, toasted
    120 g (1 cup)
UNSALTED BUTTER 100 g
    (½ cup)
SUGAR granulated 210 g
    (1 cup)
EGGS 100 gr (2 eggs)
COCOA POWDER 70 g
    (½ cup)
HONEY (1 tsp)

SALT pinch
BAKING POWDER (1 tsp)
DARK CHOCOLATE CHIPS
    120 g (¾ cup)
"00" FLOUR 300 g (2 cups)

TOPPING:
EGG WASH 1 whole egg
SUGAR sprinkle

To start this recipe, you will need to take your pistachio nuts and rinse them under water. Then lay them on a sheet pan and bake until toasted at 350°F for 8-10 minutes. Remove from oven and let them cool.

In a mixing bowl, beat butter, sugar, eggs, cocoa powder, honey, salt, and baking powder. Slowly incorporate all the ingredients together. Once they are mixed, add chocolate chips and the cooled pistachio nuts.

Now comes the fun part of it. Take a piece of the dough, and on a lightly floured surface, create a long, small sausage. Lay it in a baking pan and flatten evenly to create a bread-looking baguette. Egg-wash the top of it and sprinkle with a little bit of granulated sugar. Bake at 350°F for 15 minutes and let it cool down. Now, with a chef's knife, cut ¾-inch-thick slices at a 30-degree angle. Lay them on the pan with the pistachio facing up. Bake again for no more than 5 minutes.

I like my chocolate biscotti not too crunchy; therefore, I cook them for only 2 more minutes.

SABLÉE (crumbly and "sandy" cookie or crust)

The sablée cookies are delicious. Sablées are made of a mixture of butter (which must be of excellent quality to release all its aroma), sugar, and flour. The dough does not include eggs, but the presence of butter and sugar makes these cookies sandy, with a crumbly and gritty texture, as the name suggests.

Cookie sablées are of French origin and can be flavoured with cinnamon or other spices, or they can be prepared with salted butter to create a contrast of sweet and salty. Truly unique!

UNSALTED BUTTER 120 g (½ cup)
"00" FLOUR 200 g (1 ⅓ cups)
VANILLA BEAN SEEDS, extracted 1 pod
LEMON ZEST (½ lemon)
ORANGE ZEST (½ orange)
SALT 1 pinch
EGG YOLKS 35 g (2 yolks)
GRANULATED SUGAR 80 g (½ cup)

SUGAR GLAZE
POWDERD SUGAR 1 ½ cups
WATER 3 tbsp

Combine butter, flour, aromas (vanilla bean seeds, lemon zest, orange zest), and salt in a mixing bowl, and beat with a pattle attachment. Then add the egg yolks. Finish by adding granulated sugar. Once the mixture is well combined, wrap it with plastic and let it rest in the fridge for 2 hours before use. After the dough is refrigerated, roll it and form a long sausage. Next, flatten the top and sides to create a cube-like form. Cut into ¼-inch slices and lay on parchment paper. Bake at 350°F for 20 minutes. Once it comes out of the oven, brush the top of the cookies with sugar glaze.

CREAMS AND CUSTARDS

Knowing how to successfully create creams and custards will turn a basic recipe into an incredible experience. These creams can be used to fill all your cakes and to create delightful pastries.

VANILLA CUSTARD

When we were little kids, my mom made us fresh vanilla custard with milk from the cows and eggs from the neighbor's farm. She put it in a coffee mug and we enjoyed it on a terrace overlooking the mountains and the fields.

> MILK 900 ml (4 cups)
> HEAVY WHIPPING CREAM 100 ml (⅓ cup)
> VANILLA BEAN SEEDS, extracted 1 pod
> SUGAR 250 g (1 ¼ cups)
> EGG YOLKS 200 g (10 yolks)
> SUGAR 90 g (½ cup)
> "00" FLOUR 90 g (½ cup)

To prepare custard on a stovetop, pour milk and heavy whipping cream into a large pot. Extract vanilla bean seeds by scraping them. Add seeds and sugar to the stove pot, and bring to boil. Meanwhile, beat egg yolks with sugar. Once the milk is boiling, put flour into the egg yolk mixture, along with a little bit of boiling milk. Once both mixtures are combined, pour the mixture into the boiling milk. Without turning off the fire, stir carefully until the cream is dense and boils again.

CHOCOLATE CREAM

Chocolate cream is one of the main characters in the pastry cream world. This cream is my Great Aunt Magda's most favourite pastry cream. She lived with me and my family. She raised us like our mom, and we always saw her as our grandma. She always used to make Torta del Nonno, which is a classic cake from Tuscany. It was her favorite.

MILK 900 ml (4 cups)
HEAVY WHIPPING CREAM
   100 ml (⅓ cup)
VANILLA BEAN SEEDS,
   extracted 1 pod
SUGAR 250 g (1 ¼ cups)

EGG YOLKS 200 g (10 yolks)
SUGAR 90 g (½ cup)
"00" FLOUR 90 g (½ cup)
DARK CHOCOLATE
   COUVERTURE (70%)
   380 g (2 cups)

To prepare chocolate cream on a stovetop, pour milk and heavy whipping cream into a large pot. Extract vanilla bean seeds by scraping them. Add seeds and sugar (250 g) to the stove pot, and bring to a boil.

Meanwhile, beat egg yolks with sugar (90 g). Once the milk is boiling, put flour into the egg yolk mixture, along with a little bit of boiling milk. Once both mixtures are combined, pour the mixture into the boiling milk. Without turning off the fire, stir carefully until the cream is dense and boils again. Remove from stovetop. Incorporate the chocolate couverture in pieces, and mix with a whisk until dissolved.

CHANTILLY CREAM

This is a classic, simple recipe used to fill cream puffs and cakes or used to lighten creams, such as custards.

> **HEAVY WHIPPING CREAM, chilled 1000 g (4 cups)**
> **SUGAR 100 g (½ cup)**
> **VANILLA BEAN SEEDS, extracted ½ of bean**

In a mixing bowl, whip chilled cream with sugar and vanilla seeds (scraped from their pod) until mixture reaches firm peaks. Once the cream is ready, use it right away or keep it in the fridge.

DIPLOMAT CREAM

This is the cream that makes up part of the recipe for my father's, Ivan's, favourite cake. It's a combination of vanilla custard and Chantilly cream. The lightness of this cream makes it perfect with either fresh fruit or chocolate.

This cream is made by combining custard with chantilly cream. It is very soft and very delicate. It is used to make a huge variety of pastries and cakes. To make it, follow the two following recipes. Make sure that every component is cold when you combine the custard with the chantilly cream.

TO MAKE THE CUSTARD:

MILK 900 ml (4 cups)
HEAVY WHIPPING CREAM
    100 ml (⅓ cup)
VANILLA BEAN SEEDS,
    extracted 1 pod

SUGAR 250 g (1 ¼ cups)
EGG YOLKS 200 g (10 yolks)
SUGAR 90 g (½ cup)
"00" FLOUR 90 g (½ cup)

To prepare custard on a stovetop, pour milk and heavy whipping cream into a large pot. Extract vanilla bean seeds by scraping them. Add seeds and sugar (250 g) to the stove pot, and bring to a boil.

Meanwhile, beat egg yolks with sugar (90 g). Once the milk is boiling, put flour into the egg yolk mixture, along with a little bit of boiling milk. Once both mixtures are combined, pour the mixture into the boiling milk. Without turning off the fire, stir carefully until the cream is dense and boils again.

TO MAKE THE CHANTILLY CREAM:

HEAVY WHIPPING CREAM, chilled 1000 g (4 cups)
SUGAR 100 g (½ cup)
VANILLA BEAN SEEDS, extracted ½ bean

In a mixing bowl, whip chilled cream with sugar and vanilla bean seeds (scraped from their pod) until mixture reaches firm peaks. Once the cream is ready, use it right away or keep it in the fridge.

COTTI IN FORNO
(cooked in the oven)

These rustic recipes are characteristic of Tuscany, the land where we come from. Fresh-baked pies are the perfect treat for breakfast or in the middle of the afternoon to accompany an espresso or cappuccino.

TORTA DELLA NONNA

One of the most simple, but most amazing pies you will ever have. This is, to me, a true representation of Italian cuisine. Simple ingredients and fresh farm products combined to perfection!!!!

For the first step, prepare shortbread and put in the refrigerator to chill.

TO MAKE SHORTBREAD:

UNSALTED BUTTER, cubed 150 g (¾ cup)
POWDERED SUGAR 100 g (¾ cup)
EGG YOLKS 2
"00" FLOUR 300 g (1 ¾ cups)
LEMON ZEST (½ lemon)
VANILLA EXTRACT 1 tsp

In a mixing bowl, use a paddle attachment to combine cubed butter and powdered sugar. Mix at lowest speed. Once the butter and sugar are fully combined, add egg yolks.Incorporate the flour all at once and mix to perfection. Flavour, finally, the pastry with lemon zest and vanilla extract. Turn out the

dough onto a work surface and knead quickly. Mash dough into a disc and wrap in waxed paper and put in refrigerator to chill.

Then prepare your fresh vanilla custard and chill until thoroughly cold.

TO MAKE THE CUSTARD:

MILK 900 ml (4 cups)
HEAVY WHIPPING CREAM 100 ml (⅓ cup)
VANILLA BEAN SEEDS, extracted 1 pod
SUGAR 250 g (1 ¼ cups)
EGG YOLKS 200 g (10 yolks)
SUGAR 90 g (½ cup)
"00" FLOUR 90 g (½ cup)

TOPPING
SLICED ALMONDS as desired
PINE NUTS as desired
POWDERED SUGAR garnish

To prepare custard on a stovetop, pour milk and heavy whipping cream into a large pot. Extract vanilla bean seeds by scraping them. Add seeds and sugar (250 g) to the stove pot, and bring to a boil. Meanwhile, beat egg yolks with sugar (90 g). Once the milk is boiling, put flour into the egg yolk mixture, along with a little bit of boiling milk. Once both mixtures are combined, pour the mixture into the boiling milk. Without turning off the fire, stir carefully until the cream is dense and boils again.

Using a rolling pin, spread your shortbread thin and form a 12-inch round shape. In order to succeed, make sure the shortbread is cold, making it much easier to form the tart. Carefully line a 9-inch aluminum tart pan with the shortbread round. Once it's chilled, pipe your custard from a pastry bag over the surface of your pie to fill completely. At this point, we will make the lattice for the top. Using a small knife, create small strips of dough and put them on top of your pie, spacing them ¼-inch apart. Repeat this step in the opposite direction to create your beautiful top.

Preheat your oven to 350°F. After 7-8 minutes, put a handful of pine nuts and sliced almonds on top. Bake until top is golden, making sure the bottom is cooked, also. If you see that the oven bakes too fast, decrease the temperature to 325°F. Once it is done, let it cool down a bit and remove from tart shell. Sprinkle some powdered sugar on top and enjoy while it is still warm. Buon appetito!!!!!

CHOCOLATE AND PEAR PIE

This cake is my brother Massimiliano's great recipe. The delicacy of the pears, cut down with dark chocolate and combined with the buttery and nutty flavour of almonds, makes this cake one of the greatest I have ever eaten or made.

SHORTBREAD CRUST (BOTTOM CRUST)
DARK CHOCOLATE COUVERTURE (70%) 70 g (½ cup)
PEARS 3 (Peeled and halved)
MILK 1 ltr (5 cups)
VANILLA BEAN SEEDS, extracted 1 pod

SBRICIOLONA CRUST (TOP CRUST)
UNSALTED BUTTER 100 g (½ cup)
SUGAR 100 g (½ cup)
ALMOND FLOUR 100 g (½ cup)
"00" FLOUR 100 g (½ cup)

TOPPING
POWDERED SUGAR AND COCOA
POWDER sprinkle

Let's start by preparing the shortbread (see recipe for Pasta Frolla at page 4) for the bottom crust of a 9-inch tart shell. Bake for no more than 10 minutes at 350F and then set aside. Melt down the dark chocolate. Once it is liquid, pour chocolate on the bottom of the shortbread tart. This will work as a layer to protect the crust from the pear juice's tendency to make your crust soggy. Cook your pears in a bath of milk and fresh vanilla bean until soft. Then chop pears and layer them on top of the chocolate. To finish the pie, let's make some Sbriciolona Crust.

SBRICIOLONA CRUST:

In a mixer, combine butter, sugar, almond flour, and "00" flour. Beat everything until it looks like crumbs. If you over mix it, you will make a cookie dough that will not have the consistency needed for the crust. Once it's ready, crumble it on top of the pie to cover. Preheat the oven to 350°F. Bake for 25-30 minutes. Cool down pie and remove from mold. Sprinkle powdered sugar and cocoa powder on top before serving.

TORTA DI RICOTTA

Simple and fresh ingredients, such as ricotta cheese and lemon, reminds me of the best of Mediterranean flavours from southern Italy.

SHORTBREAD CRUST
DARK COUVERTURE CHOCOLATE (64%),
    melted 70 g (½ cup)
RICOTTA CHEESE 750 g (2 ½ cups)
EGGS 4-5
POWDERED SUGAR 170 g (1 ¼ cups)
LEMON ZEST 1 whole
HEAVY CREAM 100 g (½ cup)

Prepare shortbread crust to cover a 9-inch round, 2-inch high pie pan (see recipe for Pasta Frolla on page 4).

Pour your melted chocolate onto the pie crust. In a mixing bowl, combine your fresh ricotta cheese, eggs, powdered sugar, and lemon zest. Mix everything until nice and smooth. Once ready, add your heavy cream. Then pour your mixture into your pie, leaving at least ½-inch from the top of the crust; otherwise, it will rise over the edges of the pan while baking. Bake at 325°F for at least 35 minutes or until it sets and the top starts to get brown. If you notice your pie cracking, turn the temperature down to 300°F to avoid drying. Serve your pie at room temperature and sprinkle with some powdered sugar.

TORTA DI MELE

The apple pie is a classic dessert, prepared all over the world that has, over time, taken the characteristic of the place in which it is prepared. The use of apples in sweets has virtually spread everywhere, so we can find the American apple pie or the nearest strudel. Torta di Mele is very simple and quick to prepare, and the result is a cake that remains soft and creamy.

APPLES 700 g 4-5 apples
LEMON, juiced 1
EGGS 2
SUGAR 200 g (1 cup)
UNSALTED BUTTER, melted
    100 g (½ cup)
LEMON ZEST 1 whole lemon
CINNAMON 1 tsp
MILK 200 ml (1 cup)

BAKING POWDER 1 tsp
VANILLA BEAN SEEDS,
    extracted 1 pod
SALT 1 pinch
"00" FLOUR 200 g (1 ¼ cups)
POWDERED SUGAR AND
    CINNAMON as needed
    for topping

Peel the apples. Cut into slices and place them in a container with lemon juice; this will prevent the apple from darkening.

Using a hand-held whisk, mix the eggs with the sugar. When ingredients are completely combined, add melted butter. Gradually combine all the other ingredients: lemon zest, cinnamon, milk, baking powder, vanilla bean seeds (scraped from the pod), and a pinch of salt. Lastly, pour in the flour and stir very well so you get a smooth mixture that is not too liquid. Combine with apples drained from the lemon juice. Stir to scatter apples. Butter and flour a 9-inch cake pan and pour in the mixture. Sprinkle the surface with powdered sugar mixed with cinnamon. Bake in oven preheated to 350°F for 50-60 minutes. To serve, sprinkle the surface again with more powdered sugar mixed with cinnamon.

Typically sweet apples used in this recipe are: the Golden, thin-skinned, deep yellow gold, with soft, juicy, fragrant pulp; the Fuji, red light-to-dark-green-on-yellow skinned, with crisp, juicy, sweet flesh, sour and aromatic; the Royal Gala, two-tone, red and yellow, a fine, crisp, juicy sweet taste.

TORTA PARADISO

This torta was born in Pavia, Italy, in 1878, in the pastry shop of Enrico Vigoni. Legend has it that after several tests, Enrico Vigoni did a taste test with the end result of a noblewoman's instinctual response: "This cake is paradise." This sweet pastry soon became a symbol of Pavia and a classic of Italian pastry: a mix of simple ingredients that are a reminder of sponge cake but with the added presence of butter and the addition of baking powder for an extremely soft result. Lightweight, high, and crumbly, this heavenly cake is as soft as a cloud. Fasten your aprons and get ready to enjoy this recipe, "Paradise."

UNSALTED BUTTER 100 g (½ cup)
POWDERED SUGAR 100 g (¾ cup)
VANILLA BEAN SEEDS, extracted 1 pod
LEMON ZEST 1 whole lemon
SALT 1 pinch
EGGS 50 g 1 egg
EGG YOLKS 125 g (6 yolks)
"00" FLOUR 65 g (⅓ cup)
POTATO STARCH 50 g (⅓ cup)
BAKING POWDER 1 tsp

In a mixer, whip butter until creamy with powdered sugar, aromas (extracted vanilla bean seeds, lemon zest), and salt. Combine the whole egg without slowing the mixing speed. Continue to mix and incorporate the yolks, too. Once this is done, you should have an airy, soft mixture. Slowly fold in your previously sifted dry ingredients (flour, potato starch, baking powder), scraping from the bottom of the bowl to the top. Over-mixing will result in a very dense cake. Butter a 9-inch pie pan and fill ¾ full with the batter. Bake at 350°F for at least 30 minutes. With a toothpick, poke the center of the cake, and if it is dry, your cake will be ready.

TORTA DI VERDURE

The typical cuisine of Lucca, my city, is one of the tastiest of Tuscany. The delicious tordelli, the delicious soups, the traditional buccellato, and many other delicacies delight the most discerning palates. Torta di Verdure is a pastry shell shaped like a crown filled with vegetables and spices, resulting in a fascinating balance between sweet and salty. A sweet cake of vegetables? Yes, and I assure you it is exquisite. Make it and you will see!

CRUST:
UNSALTED BUTTER, cubed 150 g (¾ cup)
POWDERED SUGAR 100 g (¾ cup)
EGG YOLKS 2
"00" FLOUR 300 g (2 cups)
LEMON ZEST ½ lemon
VANILLA EXTRACT 1 tsp

FILLING:

RICE ARBORIO 100 g (½ cup)

WATER 200 ml (¾ cup)

MILK 200 ml + a bit for the bread (1 cup)

SUGAR 120 g + 1 Tbsp for the rice (½ cup)

BREADCRUMBS 100 g (1 cup)

UNSALTED BUTTER 50 g (¼ cup)

CHARD, 1 bunch

PARSLEY (finely chopped), a handful

PARMIGIANO CHEESE, grated 1 Tbsp

PINENUTS 100 g (½ cup)

RAISINS 50 g (⅓ cup)

CINNAMON AND NUTMEG a pinch of each

EGGS 2

SALT AND PEPPER a pinch of each

PREPARE THE CRUST:

In a mixing bowl, use a hook attachment to combine cubed butter and powdered sugar. Mix at lowest speed. Once the butter and sugar are fully combined, add egg yolks. Incorporate the flour all at once and mix to perfection. Flavour, finally, the pastry with lemon zest and vanilla extract. Turn out the dough onto a work surface and knead quickly. Mash dough into a disc and wrap in waxed paper. Let it cool down in the refrigerator, then place in 9" cake pan.

PREPARE THE FILLING:

Prepare the filling by cooking the rice with water, milk, and a tablespoon of sugar until it has absorbed all the liquid, about half an hour. Soak breadcrumbs in a little bit of milk. In a skillet, melt butter and sauté the finely chopped chard. Remove from heat, and add the parsley and parmigiano cheese. Transfer vegetables to a bowl. Add rice arborio and breadcrumbs to mix. Add squeezed breadcrumbs, pine nuts, raisins, and a little cinnamon. Combine nutmeg, sugar, and eggs. Mix well. Pour mixture into the crust and form the edge of the dough into small beaks, because a vegetable cake without beaks does not exist! Bake for 25-30 minutes at 350°F until mixture is firm and crust is nice and golden.

PASTICCERIA MIGNON
(bite-sized pastries)

Bite-sized pastries are becoming increasingly pop-ular. These small bites of indulgence are the most common thing you will want to make for your next party, and your friends and family will love the chance to choose from different flavours.

BIGNÉ ALLO ZABAIONE

Zabaione cream is one of the most classic and popular: it is prepared by beating the egg yolks and sugar, generally enriched with dry Marsala, and then baked in a water bath until it becomes thick and frothy.

Let's start by making our pâte à choux:

> WATER 200 ml (¾ cup)
> UNSALTED BUTTER, cubed 100 g (½ cup)
> SALT 1 pinch
> "00" FLOUR 125 g (½ cup + ⅓ cup)
> EGGS 4-5

Bring the water, cubed butter and salt to boil in a saucepan. Add flour all at once. Cook to dry the mixture, stirring briskly, until a tight dough forms and pulls away from the pan. Pour the mixture in a mixing bowl with a paddle attachment.

Incorporate eggs slowly, 1 by 1.

Place round half-balls on a greased pan using a pastry bag. Bake for 15 minutes at 350°F or until golden. Set aside.

Let's move on to the zabaione cream.

ZABAIONE CREAM

> EGGS 8
> SUGAR 160 g (¾ cup)
> MARSALA WINE, sweet 100 ml (⅜ cup)
> FONDANT ICING, white 50 g (½ cup)
> PINK FOOD COLOR 1 drop

Separate the yolks from 8 eggs (you will not need the whites). Place yolks and sugar in a steel bowl that has a handle and a thick bottom (which must be placed in a water bath). Beat with a whisk (or electric mixer) until an airy, foamy, smooth, almost-white cream forms. Gradually combine the wine, always beating to absorb the liquid. When all the ingredients are well blended, dip the pan in a water bath inside a larger pot, filled to ⅓ with hot water; the fire must be very low, and the water must never boil, but rather must maintain a slight shudder. Stir with a whisk for about 10-15 minutes, until you see the cream swell, thicken, and become smooth. At this point, you can remove the zabaione from the heat and let it cool, continuing to mix until completely chilled; otherwise, the wine will separate from the mixture.

At this point, put the zabaione cream into a pastry bag that has a metal tip. Poke a hole with the pastry tip into the bottom of our pâte à choux cream puff and fill it.

Melt down some sugar icing with a few drops of water and add pink food color.

Decorate your cream puff by using a pastry bag and creating a nice top.

CANNOLI DI RICOTTA

This is a classic dessert born in Sicilia, an island south of Italy. Cannoli di Ricotta was originally made during the region's carnival. It later became an everyday dessert throughout the year.

24 cannoli
RICOTTA CHEESE 750 g (3 cups)
"00" FLOUR 250 g (1 ½ cups)
SALT 1 pinch
CINNAMON 1 pinch
COFFEE POWDER 1 pinch
COCOA POWDER 5 g (1 tsp)
POWDERED SUGAR 30 g (1 tsp)
LARD OR UNSALTED BUTTER 50 g (1 tsp)
EGG 1
WHITE WINE VINEGAR 30 ml (1 tsp)
MARSALA WINE, dry 30 ml (1 tsp)
SUGAR 300 g (1 ½ cups)
DARK CHOCOLATE CHIPS 75 g (½ cup)
CANDIED ORANGE 75g (½ cup)

GARNISH
PISTACHIO NUTS as needed
CHOCOLATE CHIPS as needed
POWDERED SUGAR as needed

Before starting preparation on the shells, put the ricotta cheese in a colander. Place colander (containing ricotta) into a bowl to drain in the fridge.

TO PREPARE THE SHELLS:

Sift together flour, salt, cinnamon, powdered coffee, cocoa powder, and powdered sugar. Add lard (or butter), egg, and vinegar mixed with the Marsala wine; these liquids must be added slowly because it might not be necessary to add them entirely, depending on how the flour absorbs. Keep in mind that the dough should be soft and flexible but firm, a bit harder than bread dough. Knead the mixture for 5 minutes on a work surface until it is elastic, smooth, and homogeneous. Wrap, using plastic wrap and put it to rest for at least an hour in the fridge.

NOW PREPARE THE CREAM FOR THE TOPPING:

Place the well-drained ricotta cheese into a bowl, and add sugar. Gently stir the ingredients without mixing too much. Cover the bowl with plastic wrap and place in refrigerator for at least an hour. Once you have a very fine cream, add chocolate chips and candied orange.

Keep the ricotta cheese mixture in the refrigerator in a lidded container.

Pull the cannoli shell dough into a thin 2.1-mm thickness (you can use a dough sheeter or pull it with a rolling pin). Using round pastry rings with a diameter of 9 cm, draw at least 24 shapes that you will pull with your hands to make into ovals. Roll onto metal cylinders, taking care to brush the ends with egg white before stacking.

Heat lard (or oil) in a saucepan (not too big) until you get to 350-375°F, and fry all the shells. Put them on a couple of sheets of absorbent paper to drain excess oil. Allow to cool completely before removing metal cylinders.

Once the shells are cold, fill them with ricotta cheese mixture that you pipe from a pastry bag with a plain, wide nozzle. Decorate with diced pistachio nuts on one end and chocolate chips on the other. Sprinkle with powdered sugar.

BACI DI DAMA

Lady's Kisses (almond cookies sandwiched with dark chocolate)

The name of this cookie comes from its resembling two lips kissing. Fragrant cookies combined with chocolate make this the perfect cookie to pair with a cappuccino.

UNSALTED BUTTER 100 g (½ cup)
"00" FLOUR 100 g (⅔ cup)
SUGAR 100 g (½ cup)
ALMOND FLOUR 100 g (⅔ cup)

CHOCOLATE GANACHE:
HEAVY WHIPPING CREAM 250 ml (1 cup)
UNSALTED BUTTER 30 g less than (¼ cup)
DARK COUVERTURE CHOCOLATE (64 %) 250 g (1 ½ cup)

In a mixing bowl, combine butter, flour, sugar, and almond flour.

Beat until combined. Let it rest for 30 minutes in the fridge.

Once the dough is chilled, form round balls. Bake 20 minutes at 350°F.

The balls will become half-domes after cooked.

Now let's start the chocolate ganache:

In a small stove pot, warm up the heavy whipping cream with the butter. When it is hot, drop the chocolate into it and melt it down until almost boiling.

Remove from stove and let cool for 10 minutes. Then mix the ingredients until it becomes whipped.

Using a star tip in a pastry bag, pipe the flat side of the cookie and combine with another one.

OCCHIO DI BUE (shortbread cookie)

Named for their bulls' eye shape, these cookies are delicious pastries with a soft filling of jam. They take their name from their shape, also reminiscent of an egg cooked sunny-side up. They're simple to prepare and impressive. They can be made with different shapes: circles, flowers, hearts, in short, anything you like that is well shaped for filling with jam, chocolate, or hazelnut chocolate spread.

> SHORTBREAD recipe page 4
> CHOCOLATE HAZELNUT SPREAD as needed to fill cookies
> POWDERED SUGAR garnish

Start by preparing the shortbread (page 4):

Roll out some of the dough (⅛ inch thick) between 2 sheets of wax paper (keep remaining dough chilled). If dough becomes too soft to roll out, rewrap in plastic and chill until firm. Cut out as many cookies as possible from dough with larger cookie cutter and transfer to 2 ungreased large baking sheets, arranging them about 1 inch apart. Using a smaller cookie cutter, cut out centers from half of the cookies, reserving centers and rerolling along with the scraps. Bake cookies at 350°F, switching the position of the sheets halfway through baking, until edges are golden, about 15 minutes total.

Let shortbread cookies cool down and then prepare to fill them.

In Italy, Occhio di Bue cookies are very popular filled with chocolate hazelnut spread.

Fill a pastry bag with chocolate hazelnut spread and pipe some of it in the center of a large cookie. Sprinkle powdered sugar on the cookie with the hole and place it in the center of a large cookie with the hazelnut spread.

FUNGHETTI AL CIOCCOLATO (chocolate mushrooms)

What I like about this dessert is that it reminds me of my Grandpa Romano. We have a house in the mountains where we used to go and spend time every year. My grandpa has a forest, and he took me and my brother picking all sorts of fresh mushrooms, such as porcini and galletti.

Prepare the pâte à choux dough and pour it into a pastry bag.

PÂTE À CHOUX
WATER 200 ml (1 cup)
UNSALTED BUTTER, cubed 100 g (½ cup)
SALT 1 pinch

> "00" FLOUR 125 g (½ cup +3 Tbsp)
> EGGS 4-5

Bring the water, cubed butter, and salt to a boil in a saucepan. Add flour all at once. Cook to dry the mixture, stirring briskly, until a tight dough forms and pulls away from the pan. Pour the mixture into a mixing bowl with a beater attachment.

Incorporate eggs slowly, 1 by 1.

Create small cream puffs for the heads of the mushrooms, as well as small éclairs with a pointy end for the body of the mushrooms.

Bake at 350°F for 20 minutes or until golden.

In the meantime, prepare a chocolate custard by using the following recipe.

CHOCOLATE CUSTARD

> MILK 900 ml (4 cups)
> HEAVY WHIPPING CREAM 100 ml (⅓ cup)
> VANILLA BEAN SEEDS, extracted 1 pod
> SUGAR 250 g (1 ¼ cups)
> EGG YOLKS 200 g (10 yolks)
> SUGAR 90 g (½ cup)
> "00" FLOUR 90 g (½ cup)
> DARK CHOCOLATE COUVERTURE (70%) 380 g (2 cups)

To prepare chocolate cream on a stovetop, pour milk and heavy whipping cream into a large pot. Extract vanilla bean seeds by scraping them. Add seeds and sugar (250 g) to the stove pot, and bring to a boil.

Meanwhile, beat egg yolks with sugar (90 g). Once the milk is boiling, put flour into the egg yolk mixture, along with a little bit of boiling milk. Once both mixtures are combined, pour the mixture into the boiling milk. Without turning off the fire, stir carefully until the cream is dense and boils again. Remove from stovetop. Incorporate the chocolate couverture in pieces, and mix with a whisk until dissolved.

TO FINISH:

CHOCOLATE CUSTARD 200 g (½ cup)
WHIPPED CREAM 40 g (¼ cup)
POWDERED SUGAR garnish
COCOA POWDER garnish

Once the custard is cold, add 20 percent of the whipped cream. Combine the two together and pipe it into both the cream puff and the éclair from underneath.
Then put the body inside the cream puff so it will resemble a little mushroom.
Dust with powdered sugar and a touch of cocoa powder.
Serve fresh or preserve in the fridge.

CROSTATINA DI FRUTTA (small fruit tart)

My favorite dessert is definitely a fresh fruit tart that combines fruit, cream, and a light, buttery crust. When I was growing up in Italy, I had a field with fresh fruits and vegetables across the street from my house. Cows grazed on the other side of the field on the farm that also raised chickens and eggs. My mom made this dessert for almost all my birthdays.

> **SHORTBREAD**
> **DIPLOMAT CREAM** see recipe page 24
> **FRESH SEASONAL FRUITS**

Start by making shortbread (page 4), and chill it for 30 minutes. Roll shortbread with a rolling pin to the desired thickness. Cut out circles and put them inside aluminum mini tart shells. Bake at 350°F for 18 minutes.
Once the shortbread is cooled, remove from shell.
Now prepare a diplomat cream following all the steps delicately.
Once the cream is ready, fill a pastry bag with a round tip.
You can now top the tart with fresh berries, strawberries, figs or any fruit that is in season.

L'ARTE DEL GELATO
(art of gelato)

As good Italian people, we could not neglect instructions for real, fresh homemade gelato. Gelato is a culture, a lifestyle, and a way to refresh your senses with something sweet and creamy.

FIOR DI LATTE (the flower of milk)   (milk gelato base)

The flower of milk can be defined as the most simple gelato, but one of the most versatile. It can be used as a topper for a nice pie or as the base of your flavoured gelatos.

> MILK 500 ml (2 ½ cups)
> HEAVY WHIPPING CREAM 100 ml (⅓ cup)
> DEXTROSE 25 g (2 Tbsp)
> POWDERED MILK 25 g (2 Tbsp)
> SUGAR 120 gr (¼ cup + 2 Tbsp)
> VANILLA BEAN SEEDS, extracted 1 pod

First, put a small saucepan on the stove with milk, fresh cream, dextrose, powdered milk, and granulated sugar; stir to mix all ingredients.
Bring to a temperature of 185°F, stirring constantly.
Once the temperature is reached, turn the heat off and transfer the mixture into a bowl.
Incorporate vanilla bean seeds (scraped from vanilla bean pod). Mix well and put in refrigerator to cool.
Once the gelato is chilled, whisk to remove any lumps, and put it in the freezer. This process will take about 3 to 5 hours. Every 30 minutes, it needs to be mixed again to make a creamy gelato.

CREMA

My family and I spent many summers in Pianaccio, a very small place in the mountains located in the region of Bologna, Italy. There was a small restaurant where we used to go, and Gianni, the owner, had an antique gelato machine. He made the best crema gelato I have ever had. Right before he passed, he was so kind to share his recipe with us.

> MILK 500 ml (2 ½ cups)
> SUGAR 120 g (¼ cup + 2 Tbsp)
> DEXTROSE 25 g (2 Tbsp)
> POWDERED MILK 25 g (2 Tbsp)
> EGG YOLKS 100 g (5 yolks)
> VANILLA BEAN SEEDS, extracted 1 pod
> HEAVY WHIPPING CREAM 100 ml (⅓ cup)

Pour milk into a saucepan and add sugar, dextrose, and powdered milk. Mix and add egg yolks. Beat with a whisk.

Now, add the vanilla bean seeds (extracted from pod). Bring everything to 185°F degrees (not a degree more; eggs will coagulate, otherwise), stirring constantly. Turn off the heat and soak pan in ice water to lower the temperature; during this operation, continue stirring the mixture. When mixture is cold, put it to rest in refrigerator for at least 2 hours. Once the gelato is chilled, whisk to remove any lumps and put it in the freezer. This process will take about 3 to 5 hours. Every 30 minutes, it needs to be mixed again to make a creamy gelato.

CIOCCOLATO

Rich, dark, and extraordinary is what I like to think of the chocolate gelato.

SUGAR 160 g (¾ cup)	GLUCOSE 15 g
EGG YOLKS 120 g (6 yolks)	(1 tsp)
MILK 500 ml (2 ½ cups)	COCOA POWDER
HEAVY WHIPPING CREAM 150 ml (⅔ cup)	50 g (⅓ cup)

Using an electric mixer, combine sugar and egg yolks. Beat until yolks become clear. Place milk, cream, and glucose in a saucepan and heat. Pour milk mixture over egg yolks and stir with a whisk until all ingredients are well amalgamated. Then return to the heat and cook, stirring constantly, until it reaches a temperature of 185°F (check the temperature with a thermometer). Do not bring to a boil; otherwise, the yolks will form lumps. Remove from heat and add cocoa powder, stirring well. Cool down the mixture immediately, placing the bowl in a larger container containing ice. Refrigerate for about 1 hour. Once the gelato is chilled, whisk to remove any lumps, and put it in the freezer. This process will take about 5 hours. Every 30 minutes, it needs to be mixed again to make a creamy gelato.

FRAGOLA (strawberry)

My Uncle Vincenzo grew strawberries, and I grew up helping him plant and cover them for the harsh Italian winters. Juicy, sweet strawberries were always the perfect base for our fruit salads.

SUGAR 150 g (¾ cup)
WATER 300 ml (1 ⅓ cups)
STRAWBERRIES 500 g (about 20 strawberries)
EGG WHITE, pasteurized 50 g (2 whites)

To prepare the strawberry gelato, start by pouring sugar and water into a saucepan. Bring to a boil, mixing to make sure the sugar is completely dissolved. Blend strawberries and filter out the seeds. Pour the strawberry puree into a saucepan. Continue to boil for at least 2 minutes and then remove from fire. Let it cool down and then put in fridge to chill. Now put the strawberry mixture in a tall container and mix until everything is smooth. Beat egg whites until they are foamy. Combine the whites with the strawberry mixture and mix well. Put everything in the freezer for about 4 hours, mixing every 30 minutes.

LIMONE (lemon)

Throughout my childhood, the perfume of lemon was always a present and familiar ingredient in our Italian cuisine. This water-based, dairy-free gelato is the most refreshing of all.

SUGAR 200 g (1 cup)
WATER 300 ml (1 ⅓ cups)
LEMON ZEST 2 whole lemons
LEMON JUICE 4 whole lemons
EGG WHITE, pasteurized 50 g (2 whites)

To prepare the lemon gelato, start by pouring sugar and water into a saucepan. Bring to a boil, mixing to make sure the sugar is completely dissolved. Peel the zest of 2 whole lemons and put it right into the saucepan. Let sit for at least 2 minutes and then remove from fire. Put it in the fridge to chill. Juice lemons and add juice to the chilled mixture. With a sieve, strain everything, and put it in a tall container. Mix until smooth. Now beat the egg whites until they are foamy. Add the egg whites to the gelato and mix well. Put everything in the freezer for about 4 hours, mixing every 30 minutes.

PISTACHIO

In the south of Italy, the Bronte area of Sicilia (Sicily) is the capital of the Pistacchio di Bronte.

Also known as "green gold," the Pistacchio di Bronte represents the largest economic resource for the local town of Zafferana Etnea. Nutty and creamy, this gelato is made with this amazing nut mixed with the delicate sweetness of milk to showcase the flavours.

PISTACHIOS 100 g (1 cup)
MILK 250 ml (1 ¼ cups)
HEAVY WHIPPING CREAM 160 ml (⅔ cup)
DEXTROSE 30 g (2 Tbsp)
POWDERED MILK 20 g (2 Tbsp)
SUGAR (divided) 90 g (½ cup)
EGG YOLK 1

Toast pistachios in a hot pan. Peel and chop nuts finely until you get a paste inside the chopper. You will see the pistachios become finely ground, and then slowly you'll see the oil from the nut come out and turn the mixture into a paste. Combine milk, heavy whipping cream, dextrose, milk powder, and 60 g of sugar in a saucepan. Stir well, and bring mixture almost to a boil. While the milk mixture is heating, beat the egg yolk with the remaining sugar. Pour the hot milk mixture into the egg yolk, while stirring with a whisk. Transfer to a pot, and bring the mixture to 185°F, stirring constantly. Immediately transfer the cream into a bowl. Add pistachio paste. Emulsify everything well with an immersion blender. Then put the bowl in an ice bath to bring the mixture to room temperature. Once the mixture is chilled, whisk to remove any lumps, and put in the freezer. This process will take about 5 hours. Mix every 30 minutes to make a creamy gelato.

RICETTE DI FAMIGLIA
(Carrara Family recipes)

These recipes are all related to our family who still live back home in Italy. Each recipe represents a person that we love and care for so much. Our family is the reason I decided to share these recipes with you.

TIRAMISÚ

The origin of tiramisu comes from several legends. According to a late 1600s legend from Siena, Tuscany, a group of pastry chefs decided to make a cake for the Grand Duke Cosimo III de' Medici. The chefs wanted it to reflect the qualities of the Grand Duke, so they needed to make an important, delicious dessert, made with simple ingredients. The tiramisu was called "The Soup of the Duke." Noble people at the time liked this cake and thought it had aphrodisiac qualities.

My mom, Laura, loves coffee and chocolate. This has been a family recipe ever since I was born. The creaminess of this cake, with its pure, strong coffee taste, makes this dessert one of the most popular cakes ever created in Italy.

> EGGS, separated 6
> SUGAR, divided 120 g (½ cup + 2 Tbsp)
> MASCARPONE CHEESE 500 g (2 cups)
> DARK CHOCOLATE COUVERTURE as needed

Whip egg yolks with half of the sugar until smooth and creamy. In a separate bowl, whip egg whites with the other half of the sugar until stiff peaks form. Now in a mixer, whip the mascarpone and slowly incorporate the egg yolk mixture. By hand, gently fold in the egg whites. To finish, add chopped, dark chocolate couverture.

Cover with plastic wrap and let cool in the fridge.

Meanwhile, prepare a genoise sponge cake (which will resemble lady fingers by adding powdered sugar right before cooking.)

EGGS, room temperature 5
SUGAR 175 g (½ cup + 1 Tbsp)
VANILLA BEAN SEEDS, extracted 1 pod
SALT 1 pinch
"00" FLOUR 100 g (⅔ cup)
UNSALTED BUTTER, melted 80 g (⅓ cup)
POWDERED SUGAR as needed

Pour the eggs into a mixing bowl. Add sugar, vanilla bean seeds (scraped from the pod), and pinch of salt. Mix at medium-to-high speed for at least 8 minutes while warming the outside of the bowl with a flame torch without burning the batter. This will allow our ingredients to rise and to incorporate air, which is the most important part of our sponge. Sift flour into the mixture, folding gently. Take out 10 percent of the mixture and combine it with melted butter (butter needs to be liquid but not hot). Once the butter is combined, finish by folding into the rest of the mixture. At this point, onto a sheet pan previously oiled and lined with parchment paper you can choose to make one large sponge cake or you can fill a pastry bag with your genoise mixture and pipe out lady fingers. Once the genoise had been poured or piped onto the sheet pan cover in sifted powdered sugar. Bake in the oven at 450°F for 4-5 minutes.

After the cake is done, remove immediately from pan. Prepare the coffee and add a little bit of sugar to taste. In a glass container, start layering the genoise soaked with coffee. Pour tiramisu mixture over the cake layer. Repeat layering with the genoise 2 more times. Finish the top with sprinkled cocoa powder.

COFFEE as needed
COCOA POWDER as needed

PAN DI SPAGNA RUM E CREMA

This is my father's, Ivan's, favourite dessert. His birthday cake always has to have fresh cream, rum, and fruit. He has very similar tastes to mine. He always likes to taste some good old rum with some chocolate. My dad is my biggest inspiration and is the person that always taught me to try as hard as possible, never stop, and if I make a mistake, to put my head down and start again. Perseverance is the key to success!! Start by making your sponge cake, and let it cool down.

VANILLA BEAN SEEDS, extracted 1 pod
EGGS 5
SALT 1 pinch
SUGAR 150 g (¾ cup)
"00" FLOUR 75 g (⅓)
POTATO STARCH 75 g (⅓ cup + 1 Tbsp)
Option: add orange zest to recipe.

To prepare the sponge cake, cut vanilla bean and remove seeds. Combine eggs, pinch of salt, sugar, and vanilla bean seeds (option: flavour additionally with orange zest). Whip for at least 10 minutes at medium speed until mixture is puffy, light, and fluffy. Add sifted flour and potato starch. Fold into egg mixture with a spatula very carefully from the bottom to the top, making sure the air in the mixture doesn't disappear. Grease and flour a 9-inch pan if you want a high sponge cake (otherwise use a 10-inch pan for a larger, slightly lower cake) and pour in the mixture. Flatten the batter with a spatula. Bake at 350°F for 30-35 minutes. Then prepare the diplomat cream (recipe on page 24) by preparing your custard first. Always chill the ingredients before mixing.

TO ASSEMBLE THE CAKE:

WATER 500 ml (2 ¼ cups)
SUGAR 250 (1 cup)
RUM 750 ml (3 ¼ cups)
STRAWBERRIES, thinly sliced 6
RASPBERRIES 1 cup
BLUEBERRIES 1 cup
STRAWBERRIES, halved 1 cup
WHITE CHOCOLATE COUVERTURE 4 oz (1 cup)
EDIBLE FLOWERS optional

Bring water and sugar to a boil in a saucepan. Let cool, and add rum.

Place a baking sheet in the freezer to chill.

Split the cake in half. Brush the bottom half with the rum liqueur mixture, using a pastry brush. Pipe the diplomat cream to cover the surface within ¼ inch of the edge. Scatter the surface with sliced strawberries, half of the raspberries, and half of the blueberries. Top with the other half of the cake. Pipe the top with an even layer of the diplomat cream and smooth the surface with a small offset spatula.

Microwave white chocolate couverture at 15-20-second intervals, stirring between each interval, until almost completely melted. Remove when you can still see pieces of the chocolate. Continue to stir until chocolate is completely smooth. Remove the baking sheet from the freezer, and spread out 2 thin strips of chocolate, each about ¹⁄₁₆ inch thick, 3 inches wide, and 15 inches long (they can be slightly tapered at either end). Place back in the freezer for just 1 or 2 minutes until white chocolate is set but still pliable. Once the chocolate is set, start at one end of a strip and use the edge of an offset spatula to lift and ease up the chocolate. Wrap around the edge of the cake. Repeat with the second strip so that the ends overlap.

Cut the remaining strawberries in half. Garnish the top of the cake with the remaining raspberries and blueberries, the halved strawberries, and edible flowers (optional).

TORTA ROSITA

ALKERMES LIQUEUR

The creation of the Alkermes liqueur seems to be the telling of a fairy tale. This sweet, red liqueur was created by monks in Florence, Italy, as early as the 15th century. The monks lived and worked at the Santa Maria Novella basilica in a converted cloister that functioned as an apothecary--what is now considered one of the oldest pharmacies in the world. The pharmacy, originally a workshop for creating health remedies, eventually became known for its perfumes and liqueurs. The pharmacy's fame was solidified in the 1600s when the monks created a fragrance to celebrate the marriage of fourteen-year-old Catherine de Medici's wedding. The Medici family particularly liked Alkermes liqueur, and the recipe was finally recorded in 1743 by Fra Cosimo Bucelli, then director of the pharmacy. Alkermes is made from extracts of herbs and spices, such as rose water, orange blossom water, cinnamon, vanilla, nutmeg, and coriander. The ruby color comes from crushed cochineal, or ladybugs. The red color gives the liqueur its name, from the Arabic word "qirmiz," meaning "of scarlet color."

Santa Maria Novella liqueurs and fragrances are still in production today, and the Santa Maria Novella church is currently open as a museum. Ordering information is available on the Santa Maria Novella website: http://www.sm-novella.it/catalogo.html?path=CTG-CTM004,CTG-CTM004-0,OBJ-PRD167

My little Grandma Rosita is the kindest person I know. She loves life, she loves flour, and she loves to make this cake. When I was a kid, I used to eat this cake without the alcohol. But after growing up, I finally got to try the real Torta Rosita. Chocolate, cream, and liqueur in beautiful harmony!!!

VANILLA BEAN SEEDS, extracted 1 pod	SALT 1 pinch
SUGAR 150 g (¾ cup)	POTATO STARCH 75 g (½ cup)
"00" FLOUR 75 g (½ cup) EGGS 5	Option: add orange zest to recipe.

Start by making a sponge cake. To prepare the sponge cake, cut vanilla bean and remove seeds. Combine eggs, pinch of salt, sugar, and vanilla bean seeds (option: flavour additionally with orange zest). Whip for at least 10 minutes at medium speed until mixture is puffy, light, and fluffy. Add sifted flour and potato starch. Fold into egg mixture with a spatula very carefully from the bottom to the top, making sure the air in the mixture doesn't disappear. Grease and flour a 9-inch pan if you want a high sponge cake (otherwise use a 10-inch pan for a larger, slightly lower cake) and pour in the mixture. Flatten the batter with a spatula. Bake at 350°F for 30-35 minutes. Once the sponge cake is cooked, remove from oven and let it cool.

SPONGE CAKE (recipe page 2)	SUGAR 150 gr (¾ cup)
ALKERMES LIQUEUR 200 ml (1 cup)	CHOCOLATE CUSTARD 300 g (1 cup)
WATER 300 ml (1 ¼ cups)	VANILLA CUSTARD 300 g (1 cup)
	DARK CHOCOLATE 100 g (½ cup)

To make the Alkermes solution, bring water and sugar to a boil, and once it is cooled, add the Alkermes liqueur. Cut sponge cake into pieces and soak it with Alkermes solution.

Next, prepare a chocolate custard and a vanilla custard.

In a large glass pan, layer the sponge cake soaked with the liqueur solution. Using a pastry bag, pipe the vanilla custard. Again, layer the sponge cake and pipe the chocolate custard this time.

Continue to layer in intervals until reaching the top. Finish with finely chopped dark chocolate.

TORTA DEL NONNO

This is my grandpa's favourite cake, as its Italian name suggests ("nonno" is Italian for "grandfather"). Chocolate inside a buttery crust, fresh, warm out the oven, with a cup of coffee and the newspaper, is how my grandpa liked to start his day.

For the first step, prepare shortbread and put in the refrigerator to chill.

TO MAKE SHORTBREAD:

UNSALTED BUTTER, cubed 150 g (¾ cup)
POWDERED SUGAR 100 g (¾ cup)
EGG YOLKS 2

> "00" FLOUR 300 g (1 ¾ cups)
> LEMON ZEST (½ lemon)
> VANILLA EXTRACT 1 tsp

In a mixing bowl, use a paddle attachment to combine cubed butter and powdered sugar. Mix at lowest speed. Once the butter and sugar are fully combined, add egg yolks.

Incorporate the flour all at once and mix to perfection.

Flavour, finally, the pastry with lemon zest and vanilla extract (or vanilla).

Turn out the dough onto a work surface and knead quickly. Mash dough into a disc and wrap in waxed paper and put in refrigerator to chill.

Then prepare your fresh chocolate custard and chill until thoroughly cold.

TO MAKE THE CHOCOLATE CUSTARD:

> MILK 900 ml (4 cups)
> HEAVY WHIPPING CREAM 100 ml (⅓ cup)
> VANILLA BEAN SEEDS, extracted 1 pod
> SUGAR 250 g (1 ¼ cups)
> EGG YOLKS 200 g (10 yolks)
> SUGAR 90 g (½ cup)
> "00" FLOUR 90 g (½ cup)
> DARK CHOCOLATE COUVERTURE (70%) 380 g (2 cups)

To prepare chocolate cream on a stovetop, pour milk and heavy whipping cream into a large pot. Extract vanilla bean seeds by scraping them. Add seeds and sugar (250 g) to the stove pot, and bring to a boil.

Meanwhile, beat egg yolks with sugar (90 g). Once the milk is boiling, put flour into the egg yolk mixture, along with a little bit of boiling milk. Once both mixtures are combined, pour the mixture into the boiling milk. Without turning off the fire, stir carefully until the cream is dense and boils again. Remove from stovetop. Incorporate the chocolate couverture in pieces, and mix with a whisk until dissolved.

TOPPING
SLIVERED ALMONDS as desired
70% DARK CHOCOLATE CHIPS as desired
POWDERED SUGAR garnish
COCOA POWDER garnish

Using a rolling pin, spread your shortbread thin and form a 12-inch round shape.

In order to succeed, make sure the shortbread is cold, making it much easier to form the tart. Carefully line a 9-inch aluminum tart pan with the shortbread round.

Once it's chilled, pipe your custard from a pastry bag over the surface of your pie to fill completely.

At this point, we will make the lattice for the top. Using a small knife, create small strips of dough and put them on top of your pie, spacing them ¼-inch apart. Repeat this step in the opposite direction to create your beautiful top.

Preheat your oven to 350°F. After 7-8 minutes, put a handful of slivered almonds and chocolate chips on top.

Bake until top is golden, making sure the bottom is cooked, also.

If you see that the oven bakes too fast, decrease the temperature to 325°F.

Once it is done, let it cool down a bit and remove from tart shell.

Sprinkle some powdered sugar and cocoa powder on top and enjoy while it is still warm.

Buon appetito!!!!!

CAPUTO FLOUR OF NAPLES

http://caputoflour.com/

ITALYDEPOT.COM

http://www.italydepot.com/farina-caputo-00-flour-2-2-lbs-free-shipping/

AMAZON

http://www.amazon.com/s/?ie=UTF8&keywords=caputo+00+pizzeria+flour&tag=googhydr-20&index=grocery&hvadid=33051948728&hvpos=1t1&hvexid=&hvnetw=g&hvrand=4211295674446352882&hvpone=&hvptwo=&hvqmt=b&hvdev=c&ref=pd_sl_3h4r45y49h_b